■ ■■ ■ Black Dog Publishing London New York

I'LL KEEP THINKING

nick crosbie   inflate

CONTENTS

FUN FUNCTIONAL AND AFFORDABLE

Alexander Payne

I think we all would agree with Nick Crosbie, the design director of Inflate, that the idea of turning kitchen products into little people and putting eyes on them is a bit dodgy. Crosbie is aware that his designs, the big and small products made by Inflate, are more than little people. Yes, they do add humour to banal everyday tasks, such as popping your fruit into an Inflate fruit bowl, reaching for a toothpick or putting a little light on a subject. But it's the way he does this. He wants the humour, but is simultaneously exploring and pushing processes and materials to their limit. His designs are thought through and calculated. Inflate is not a design brand which produces another table for the market because they feel like it – there has to be some exploration of benefit or process to justify putting such a common object into the marketplace.

I am sure he would smile with pride if I were to say these are truly Eamesian steps, but it's difficult to ignore the similarities. The Eames' experiments with three-dimensional moulded plywood, which initially resulted in litters and splints for the US Navy, went on to become their plywood furniture series, including such classics as the LCW (lounge chair wood) and DCM (dining chair metal). Crosbie also likes the idea of connections, the way the initial concept of a valve and blowing air into an object can be used to inflate a flip-flop to the perfect level of comfort. At the same time he is looking to create a perfect working relationship between Inflate and the manufacturer.

Inflate employ the catchphrase "Fun Functional and Affordable". They bring humour and humanity to our everyday world of designed objects. Crosbie is clear about Inflate's aim in design – "to enhance people's lives through design... their way of living".

Inflate have used processes from all areas of manufacturing, such as inflatables and high-frequency welding (armbands), dip moulding (sex toys) and rotation moulding (road bollards). They have revived these processes and in their own way revived a small sector of the British manufacturing industry through the creation of their designs. One could be forgiven for thinking that this all comes at a price, but not so with Inflate, who are always keen to point out that new ideas need not come at an extra cost.

Inflate's products are friendly – they actually make us feel happy, temporarily taking us back to the pop landscape of the 1960s. And we do, indeed, have a swell time with Inflate's products! One could also start making connections with the radical design of this period – they do all share the same goals: design for the masses. For me, though, Inflate has done away with the utopian visions dreamt up by designers such as Colombo, Superstudio and Quasar. What they have retained from this time, however, is the fun of making objects where the user is encouraged to form emotional bonds with a product. But Inflate also pose a challenge to the user – are these cheap objects of a new throw-away culture, similar to that of the 60s? In one of our interviews Crosbie related his simultaneous horror and bemusement at finding an Inflate ashtray in a bin!

The future for Crosbie is to turn Inflate into a stand-alone brand, which can become an opportunity for young designers to realise their visions by working with British manufacturing. Most important in all this is his passion for innovation and the presentation of truly bold and useful ideas. In order to do this he has created a think tank, a space for contemplation, called the 'shed' – a place in which he spends part of his working life, without telephones and other distractions of the twenty-first century.

If you listen carefully you can hear him thinking.

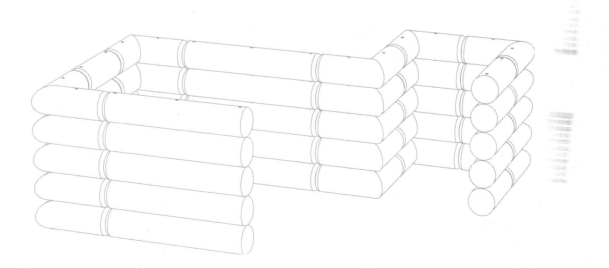

INTRODUCTION

Why designers like to live in lofts...

When I was studying in the UK there was a simple process of education to follow. O levels, A levels, HND, Foundation, Degree, Masters. Having been moderately successful at O level (many A's), I think my parents were under the impression that I was going towards a career in physics, or business studies of some sort. I did go on to physics, maths, computers and art at A level and I had also really enjoyed the rational of economics. However, I enjoyed the freedom of expression in art more. It was whilst studying these subjects that I found that I was not fully fired up for the more academic ones, nor particularly good at them. I felt that the art and graphics side suited me a lot more. I dropped all the A levels except art, and was accepted onto a Foundation course. At Foundation I was really into graphics, but I knew deep down that I was not good enough. I was unaware for some time that there was such a profession as Industrial Design. The standard education system doesn't teach you much about 3-D work, as it is mainly ceramics, with a bit of woodwork and metalwork. The worst of all is the way ceramics is seen as a girl's subject, with woodwork and metalwork for boys.

I hope it has changed now. We were not taught about design. The shocking thing is you can go through life, picking up objects and not realising that someone somewhere had to design and make the decisions and work it all out! If you actually look around you, EVERYTHING has been designed. I don't mean that everything is a designer object, more that it does not just grow on trees. It wasn't until I eventually went on to Central Saint Martin's that I realised people actually designed things.

When I became aware of my lack of ability for graphics at Foundation, I decided to try a different angle. This is when I began to work three-dimensionally. But I was still unaware of design, I was looking more at 3-D graphics.

I found there could be such a negative culture at college with students constantly moaning about facilities, etc.. I say, if you are studying design then that is what you are there for, if you want to study the internal politics of running a college then do it! It is all too easy to criticise than innovate. I just got on with things. Thinking about it, the fewer the opportunities the greater one can make of them. A lack of facilities means that you can become master of one rather the Jack of all, or should I say Jack all.

It was in the second year at Central that, amongst all the supposed starved resources, I came across an HF welder. An HF welder is a machine by which one can weld sheet PVC together to make inflatables. My interest in this machine was coupled with a need at the time to do some work. The second year at college had seen me fail too many course projects, and as a result I had been asked to re-present my portfolio at the end of the year. The next step was an obvious one – I made an inflatable folio.

It was rather crudely put together, but it did the job. With hindsight it did better than the job. When I presented it to the tutors, they loved it and allowed me to stay on. However, the thing which really stuck in my mind was that my fellow students were equally impressed. I remember thinking, this is very unusual, and attributed the success in both areas as being something to do with the emotional qualities attached to the material. I did not produce any other inflatable work whilst at the college, but my final degree show project was a waterproof floating TV, aptly named "Inflate".

It was 1993, and the recession was still not quite over so I decided to apply to the RCA. The idea to start a company called Inflate was already in the back of my mind. When I got in to the RCA I was incredibly excited – again – even more than before! Not just job for life, but a job for history. My experiences at Central Saint Martin's had taught me to take what I could from college, and the people you meet there. They can be as important as the projects you do.

Going from BA to MA was a real leap and it took me quite a while to get to grips with it. I wanted to use my time to experiment with different processes and actually spent a lot of time working with film and sound. We had a lot of projects which encouraged the cross-over of creative disciplines. So, being accepted to the RCA did me a huge favour, as it kept me from setting up Inflate too soon. It was not until I had finished my studies and had set up Inflate that I recognised the fine line in getting something right.

I knew I wanted to do Inflate, but did not quite understand how to do it or what it was. To be honest you never do. It's a bit like trying to understand the opposite sex. I didn't have any products, or even a welder at the time, but I knew I was going to do Inflate. I think I struggled a lot more at the RCA than I needed to. My obsession with starting Inflate held me back at times. I believe now that it is much better to concentrate on the subject at hand rather than be preoccupied with where you are going.

I didn't really learn until after graduating from the RCA what the course had done for me. One day (not long after graduating) I realised that I understood what I believed in in terms of design and process. I was working out who I was in terms of design – and many other things as it transpired. Post-rationalisation is a great thing! So, in a way, I would say, make as many mistakes as you can at college, build up your wealth of experiences, these will be what you draw upon in the future. My decisions were informed. I could argue them, justify them, and I could speak about why I was doing it and what I felt. But I wasn't showing people a drawing and saying, we have to make this. I was saying, this is what we need to do, this is what we need to explore, this is what we need to push. It wasn't like sitting down and saying, we need to do a cup this shape. There was no cup; no object – which was amazing. But there was a vision – I could feel it – but there were no objects. I thought, this is what it's about!

What I am saying here is that the hardest thing is to be able to define a problem and understand how to approach it. There are many different ways, no right or wrong, so how does one decide? It is not like maths. I mean, we all know 2 + 2 = 5.

Daniel Wiell was my professor at the RCA. We had a shared passion, which was HF welding, but it wasn't what we ever spoke about. I remember a meeting with him when he tried to explain what he was trying to do with all of us. He said, "What I am trying to do is give you my experiences to use or not. We are essentially trying to give you 15 years experience in two years. What we're trying to do here is to condense all this and take you on that journey." To me condense it is like a slow-play video tape, and it's not going to be such good quality. But I liked what he was saying because he wanted a situation where he saw designers getting better.

His thing was often about technology. Things like a VCR is about the technology inside it which is moving so fast that the design of its exterior doesn't go anywhere, it just reshapes. It's a superlative factor. It's purely re-styling. It is a contributing factor to the undermining of the value of the designer. With architects, they have professional qualifications, and they have to understand a lot of legal and 'structural' issues. With design, you don't have that – just your ideas and approach to problem solving. That's your professionalism. We live in a technology-driven society and design is so far behind that the design doesn't inform the development of the technology any more – it's the other way round. As a result design is being devalued as an industry because you're not adding, you're just covering. That's what Daniel was getting at. His desire to recognise that the students needed to catch him up and move ahead with their discoveries.He said, "I'm here at 36, you should be further." However, despite all the best intentions, I did see some students, who were good straight product designers, who got fucked up on that course. I think some should have finished and just got a job and not done the MA.

Whilst I was in the final year of the RCA I bought my first HF welding machine. On graduating from the school in 1995 this was going to become one of the most important investments I had ever made. But, as with every tool, it is how you use it which is the most important thing. It was with this machine that I gained the opportunity to rediscover a magic within it that had been overlooked.

Arriving in the twenty-first century there have been so many advances in manufacturing, but nothing like what happened when plastic arrived, that totally revolutionised the possibilities of manufacturing. The problem was that no one really understood the new language of this material. Initially, they were just reproducing wood or metal in plastic. Many companies threw open their doors to designers to experiment with these new materials and processes, with the likes of Verner Panton seizing the opportunity to massive effect. Verner worked with many companies developing designs, however the openness of the factories to employing designers services reduced the need to have a commercial slant on the product.

To me plastic is natural to colour. I have been into plastic ever since I started to realise what design was about. To me having the HF welding facilities in my live/work space in Old Street,

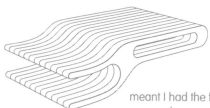

meant I had the freedom to express ideas whenever I liked. The material was cheap and the process is no more complicated than sewing. I had never really intended to do any work with the welder for my projects at the RCA. I had wanted to keep it kind of secret until I left. With hindsight this showed a lack of respect. I should have been working with my ideas at the college and embracing the conversations around the process with the tutors. Instead, I had had the welder for a few months and tried to make various products – mainly waste bins!

One day I was working on my major project, which was literally a pop-up toaster, and required an outer casing which would be pushed up and down. I decided that I would weld them in PVC in a particular form to achieve this. They were not inflated but I had some left over and so I put a valve in them and joined a few together. When inflated they started to suggest the form of a fruit bowl. I cut up a load of scrap PVC in different colours and made the complete object. It worked very well, and thus the first real product was complete.

I was now beginning to understand the language of the products and the approach to take in developing their design. It was not a case of sitting down and drawing a bubbly cartoon and expecting to make an inflatable. It was a matter of experimenting and building my own portfolio of experiences – making many mistakes along the way, coupled with happy accidents. It is about building a portfolio of observations.

With inflatable stuff, I never set out to go over past inflatable work. It was almost a stubbornness to ignore it to start with. Luckily, I feel we ignored it long enough to develop of a vision, which then reflected back. You could see where your position was, then you could benefit from other people's work and understand it on a different level. It's more interesting to look at what the Eames' did. How can you expect to recreate that? Should you expect that? I'm not saying I'm trying to, as, of course, they were the creators of some of the most important designed objects of the twentieth century. I feel, today, that's not happening now and we're missing it maybe? Today, if you look at Dunn & Raby and their Compass Table – they're concerned with the issues of the twenty-first century, like pollution, electro-magnetic stress and radio waves. That's something new, that to me is interesting – a new product that goes against the forces of the market. It's a relief that someone's coming through in this way. A lot of people would see this as art. To some people it would be shit. But I think this approach is going to transcend

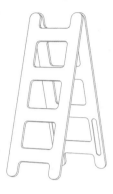

barriers.... How will it develop? What's ridiculous is that you've got companies like Ikea swamping the market and promoting themselves in a particular way. These big companies are going in the opposite direction, looking to pick up on looks, trends and fashion. They are not producing anything close to new innovative design, they're at the other end of the spectrum.

Essentially my early discoveries showed me that manufacturing moves on and becomes evermore advanced, but there are many older processes that are overlooked. In these there is the opportunity for reinvention. This is similar to what Verner was doing. However, the twenty-first century is about coupling creativity with commerce.

What is in it for me?

Initially, I drew things and tried to make them work. But the process of getting on the welder and sometimes making a mistake and then inflating it was more interesting – you'd discover things. Little secrets about the material. No matter how much time you spend drawing, you'll never discover this. It's about practical experience. It is important to recognise when an idea should not be forced. It is better not to develop than develop something which is wrong.

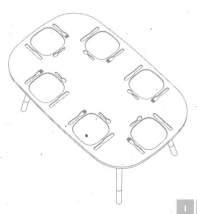

BRAND

This is a great bit of post-rationalisation. I was never really trying to develop a brand, and once you realise you are one it becomes a lot harder! I think it really was the name, the approach to the graphics, which started things.

The name Inflate came from the TV project I did whilst at college. I did not want to have a company named after a person as I felt this restricted the opportunities for others to commit design-wise, as they would always think they were working for you. The name was decided upon, and Mark and Mike Sodeau and I set up Inflate in 1995.

Whilst at college I had designed some more products after the fruit bowl, mainly a picture frame and wine rack. The picture frame had come about one evening as part of a bet to come up with and make a product in five minutes. I knew what I was going to do as soon as I started for the welder. I was detailing the design as I was cutting and preparing the material. It is all in the preparation. I say this to everyone who joins the studio. This is the art. When I first went to Japan, it was explained to me that a sushi chef spends the first two years making rice – it is one thing learning how to make the rice right, but it is

also the level of commitment to doing the mundane element and earning the right to do the good bits.

In doing Inflate it became apparent that the cost of production was going to be an issue to commercial success. Up until this point the only product we had been selling was the postcard, which was made in Camden Town. The postcards were ending up at £3.50 each and were sold through Space and American Retro. Getting the postcard made was one of the driving forces behind buying a welding machine. We had been working on other design ideas, but all the companies we spoke with to get them produced were not really interested in helping develop anything. They were only interested in the volume of production. So, having our own welding machine would open up many creative possibilities, without budget constraints.

I wanted to produce all the products in the UK. The philosophy of the company was to be "Made in Britain". I wanted a new Industrial Revolution, utilising and capitalising on overlooked manufacturing techniques and reintroducing them through new contemporary products. I liked the idea that we began exporting.

Inflate waterproof floating TV, 1993
Inflatable portfolio, 1992
Inflate logo, designed by Simon Clark, 1995

We did not have enough money, nor the commitment, to move straight to mass production. But we had our own welding machine, which meant we could produce products in small volumes as well as developing prototypes. In a way this was another of those great moments. I was able to produce prototypes which would look the same as the mass produced version of the product.

I remember making the first couple of fruit bowls in the studio. These were taken to American Retro, and sold within a day or two for £36!! The fact that I could have an idea, prototype it, and then make a couple of units for sale and get them in the shop and sold had potential. It also helped to create the illusion that the company was bigger than it actually was. Clients are a lot more comfortable in working with you if they see your products in a shop. Little did they know we had only made them a day or two earlier.

I knew all along that it would be necessary to look at full production, and all our designs were produced with that in mind. Due to the cost of production in the UK (approximately 20 times more than in the Far East) it was very important to develop all our designs so as to utilise manufacturing processes as tightly as

possible. With what I know now, production in the Far East opens up all sort of new possibilities. But I believe the fact that I was really into UK production enforced a type of constraint to our design parameters which were beneficial to the overall Inflate look we developed. Less is more, as we all know. It is very easy with inflatables to get too sickly with them if you go over the top. With the fruit bowl, for instance, we actually made it slightly smaller than prototyped to get a better weld and material yield. The design was no worse, and there was less material wastage.

Tools

Preparing the template

Cutting the material

Punching the valve hole

Welding the valve

Embossing the logo

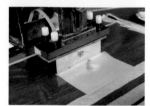

Welding the parimeter

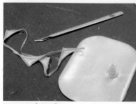

Trim out for inflate

The first HF welder, bought in 1994 for £400.

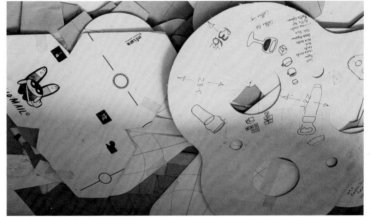

All the designs are developed using card templates These act as little stories to each product, with notes on the templates, along with visible amendments.
It is a hands on approach with the smaller objects. Each design is developed through a trial and amendment process, until they work perfectly.

We had a phone call from this guy called Tim Pyne, who was the architect working on this new show called 100% Design. I think we had looked at getting a stand there but didn't have the money. He wanted to know if we could make him a clear, funky shaped inflatable paddling pool, and in exchange they would give us free space at the show. We had not been going long at this time. We knew quite a bit about making a nice looking object, but our technical ability was not so good. Furthermore the shape of the pool did not help. Privately we realised that we would not be able to produce the object successfully, but the prospect of a free stand was too much for us and we agreed to the project.

We made the paddling pool, which was to be the centrepiece of the reception area as you entered 100% Design. In return 100% gave us a stand. On the first night of the show the pool burst, flooding the foyer. Horror! Luckily, though, our stand had been very well received, with some people even travelling from as far away as Birmingham to see it. They allowed us to stay, and Ian Rudge, the show's organiser sort of laughed off the situation. The show was the big break for Inflate. There was massive interest in our products, as well as in made to order items.

But in addition to getting a sense of how best to produce our products another opportunity fell our way. Jason Tozer, a friend I had met whilst at college, offered his photographic skills for free on our first range. Jason had been working as a professional photographer for a couple of years, and was doing really well. I could tell by the fact that he bought a couple of new CDs every week. I could not even afford more than toast with ketchup on at this time. I already knew what his day rate was and realised his investment was big. I questioned him once about how he justified what he charged, and he simply explained that he got you 115% out of your object. He took seven shots. Fee value: 14,000 pounds. Value to Inflate: priceless.

When we showed at 100% Design, as well as the interest in the products from shops and the interest in commissioned work, there was an even greater press interest. This is where the photography came in. We had more press than we could imagine. And the quality of the images from Jason often meant that we would get the bigger image on the page, including many front cover shots. This went along to help position our new brand and capitalise on the illusion that we were bigger than we actually were.

UFO light, 1996

Fruit bowl, 1995
Wine rack, 1995
Ashtray, 1995
Glasses, 1996

Sugar shaker, 1996
His & Her, 1996
Jar, 1996
Starlight, 1995

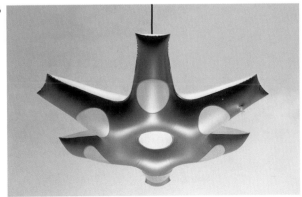

100% Design

This was the first 100% Design show, and I did not really know a lot about what it was for. To be honest, the whole industry was a new thing. When I graduated I thought that I would give Inflate a few months and then go off travelling. I did not expect the whole thing to get more and more complicated. After all the magazines I read and looked through during college, all the designers I had met, etc., etc., here we were showing at 100% Design as one of those designers.

Trade shows are a funny thing as they normally make your face grow dry – you see lots of German people walking around with electric blue, overtly angled rimmed glasses. 100% was in a tent on King's Road. The show has continued to grow and we have been a part of it all the way. The funny thing with the show is that you should never expect to take big orders there. It doesn't work that way. It is more of a 3-D advertising experience.

I have tried a whole spectrum of approaches to the show. The first year we had no money and only seven objects. The second year we went all white on a dirty green background. One year we went with just an inflatable cube which you had to go inside. I think this was the most popular stand, especially given Fiona and Laura zipping people in and out of the cube.

100% Design has rightfully put the UK back on the map of international design. The real shame is that they had to move from King's Road to Earl's Court due to growth. As an international arena Earl's Court is a pile of shite. I cannot believe that in the country we live in we cannot afford to have an arena to be proud of. I did think with the growth of the internet that people would stop needing trade shows, but the internet has actually heightened the need to have these shows. They are the opportunity to come together and exchange ideas and meet with people and clients face to face. In a way, we do much more business now through the internet, that we need the trade shows to ground ourselves once in a while.

I believe there is only so long you can have a relationship with someone until you need to meet them in person. 100% Design, for me, is like a few days in the year when I can go up the road and expect to bump into all sorts of interesting people.

1996 – this year the idea was to concentrate on the product form, so we made them all in white. The table light won the award for the best product at the show.

1998 – the show was moved to Earl's Court this year and I wasn't sure how good it would be. We participate at the last minute, but decide to approach the show with more of an art installation than a trade stand.

1999 – this show was our biggest investment made to date. The development and launch of the Memo seat, we hoped, would really lift the company to a new level.

2001 – the stand design was focussed on larger structural projects, including images of recent completed work.

2002 – Our House, designed with Idea Architects.

Starvase, 1997

85%

For me the main thing is the art of balancing what you do creatively with the business. The problem is justifying one's investments in the unknown of creativity. It is very hard for a creative person to know when to stop, as the creative process is ongoing. One of my skills has been to know, most of the time, when to stop. I never try to achieve 100% completion if the job is actually complete at 85%. It is a simple time to achievement ratio. It may take 50% of your time to achieve 85% of a project, and another 50% to achieve the final 10% with the remaining 5% never achievable.

You may remember that Jason, the photographer, offers 115% of the object in his pictures, so that coupled with the 85% gives you around 100%. The 50% of your time you save can be put towards the next 85% of the next product, thus before long you are starting to do good business with your creativity. Too many designers are too passionate about what they are doing at the expense of commercial success.

Commercial success is not a bad thing – it is a reality which we all face in this country. Commercial success gives you freedom. If you can control yourself then you can balance the business and the creativity, if not it will control you, or all goes bust!

There were little decisions made early on which were very much key moments in developing the commercial success of the brand. I met Nitzan Yaniv, a guy who had just graduated in law. He had the opportunity to join the Radisson group, but decided to give it a go with Inflate. Considering this was only four months into the business, it showed great vision on his part. This was not the obvious move for him. I knew we needed someone like this. He bought a filing cabinet!! He began to put in place a structure for the company.

We had already the notion of being partners, Mark, Mike and I. Nitzan was coming in from the outside and there was a lot of resentment from the brothers. It was becoming apparent that we would need to become a limited company, and I wanted Nitzan to be a partner. Eventually, this happened, and we were moving ahead. For the type of company we were I think our business approach, through Nitzan, was a massive strength, and it would be hard to imagine what would have happened if he did not join.

These decisions for me are the cornerstone of how we grew at the start. It is always best to get the shitty bits out the way at the start, not when you are talking about million pound companies.

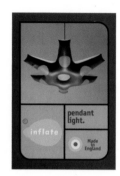

Sticker designs, 1995
Design John Kwiecinski
Photography Jason Tozer

Where my passions lay...

I remember doing a lecture with Tom Dixon early on in Antwerp. It was my first ever lecture since setting up Inflate. We were taken to this hall for dinner, which was to be proceeded by the lecture. The hall was massive, a cathedral, big enough for 400 people comfortably. I could not eat any food, I was sick with fear. We were still using slide projectors in those days, making the whole thing even more nerve racking.

Tom had spoken about how he could take an everyday object, cut it up and then sell it for thousands of pounds – how he'd created an elite object from everyday waste. I followed him, but said the opposite. My desire was to create wealth for ordinary people. I was interested in the mass market, but in a contemporary way. And I was interested in plastic moulding.

I remembered at college, whenever anyone wanted to do anything that didn't make commercial sense – clearly too expensive to make – it was always for the elite market. It's the 'excuse market'. This exclusive market for me was a thing of the past. I thought there was much more respect in designing things that hundreds of people would want. It would be a test of your ability. I have since learnt that there is also a flip side to the mass market, which is distribution and marketing.

We did a photo shoot in 1995 and I wanted to do it in front of a tower block – that was the whole thing. This was our market, a fat person with bacon and eggs. He doesn't necessarily know it's a designer product, it's there by accident. We failed successfully in not achieving this. In a way what we entered was the design-led market, with design hungry people who wanted something special, but had not been able to afford designer one-offs, buying into this new stuff at affordable prices. The brand strap line at the time was "Fun Functional and Affordable". A couple of years later we felt positioned to add "Original".

There was still only the seven products to this new brand's bow, and I was still unsure how I wanted things to move.

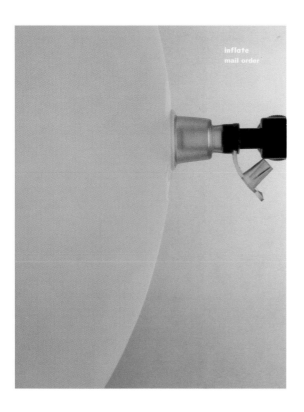

inflate
mail order

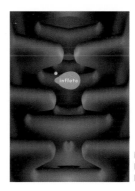

inflate

Brochure covers, 1996-1997
Design Belinda Moore
Photography Jason Tozer

Sticker designs, 1996-

Brochures, 1998

Table light, 1990

Product guidelines, 1996

Our graphic presentation has been of great importance – one of our accountants actually commented that we spent more on graphic design than some of his larger corporate clients.

Designs Simon Clark

We were going to become a brand...

We all flew out to Italy to meet Alberto Alessi. I remember having a meeting with Phillipe Starck about working on some products with him for Alessi. We had a great meeting, drinking champagne in the Thomson HQ at La Defénse. Nothing actually came of that nor subsequent meetings, however Starck did recommend to Alessi that he meet with us to review our products. The meeting went really well. Alessi has a marking system for products to assess their market potential.
It all made sense, and when the fruit bowl was put through the score system it got 9 out of 10 – 8 and above would be a very good seller.

We got given some freebies.

The long and short of the meeting was to look at developing an inflatable range for Alessi. I set about on some designs and produced a one-off folio of objects, all photographed by Jason. I was very pleased and felt this was going to do well. The only drawback was that Alessi wanted to have all the existing products as well.

Nitzan looked at the contract and we calculated that even on the best deal we would have been broke within four months, unless we came up with a totally new concept for the studio. Essentially they would have been taking all that the company had. We wanted to do new things but we could not sell the heart of the company. I realised then that we were going to have to go it alone. It was time to bolster the range and we brought out the award-winning table light, UFO light, sugar shaker, his and her mirror, and storage jar designs. And the final product in 1996 was the star vase, which was actually not inflated with air but filled with water, giving the illusion of its being inflated.

Concept designs,
presented to Alessi, 1996

dip moulded

It had become apparent that the brand needed to move on. The inflatable side was still very busy, but most of our work was in the studio and in product development for other people. The brand needed a new process. Mike and I were drifting apart. I wanted to explore what Inflate could be. I didn't just want to be a designer. I wanted to create Inflate as a springboard or platform for other designers to embrace. With that in mind I decided we needed to orchestrate a project where Inflate would work as the brand or manufacturer. I had been thinking about doing it for a while, and when I met people who I thought would be right for this, I made a mental note.

They were Michael Marriott (vase). There's a great picture of me and Michael in Cologne, standing in a fruit and veg market. He is casually standing there with a cucumber! I remember him feeling cornered as the 'recycling man'. I was saying, I'm bored of everyone thinking I just do inflatables. I explained my idea of a project allowing people the creativity to do what they liked. Michael's background in woodwork appealed to me.

Steve Bretland (piggy bank). I was good friends with him at the time. He had done rubber egg cups, which he was casting and selling himself. He was worn out by the success of these products, as he was making them himself and had no chance to design anything new. I figured it would be interesting to work with someone who had encountered the problem of success.

Michael Young (salt & pepper shakers). It was an obvious decision because I knew him really well. I wanted him to get involved because at the time he was becoming well known but hadn't yet made it. I thought he was getting confident. I thought it would be interesting to bring someone on board who could at any minute become famous. Michael always wanted to be a pop star designer, and with his boyish good looks it was all there in the making.

Mark Garside (letter holder). He was at college with me and had graduated and been working for his own company doing events and interiors. He did a lot of stuff for Vexed Generation. He did a lot of their shop interiors. I thought he would be interesting to work with because he'd studied product design, but had gone more into interiors and exhibitions. And I thought it would be interesting to get someone who hadn't done a product for production before.

Mr & Mrs Prickly, Michael Young
Piggy, Steve Bretland
Dropvase, Michael Marriot
Digital Grass, Mark Garside
all 1997

The deal was that I couldn't pay any money, but I guaranteed we'd put the design into production and show it at Frankfurt, whether I liked it or not. I thought that was a fair trade-off. That was the start of the project. We spent a long time umming and ahhing about what processes to use. I had made a list of the elements Inflate would require from a new process. These were based on things I had realised with the development of the inflatable products. One – low tech. This would mean that we would not need to spend months of learning in order to understand the process, we could therefore dedicate our time to understanding the language of the process. Two – low tooling costs. If the tooling is expensive it tends to slow down the process of development and restricts the freedom of creative expression.

I liked the idea that we could get our own prototyping machines. The thing with the HF welders for the inflatables was that having them in the studio meant that whenever you had an idea you could just test it out. If you are solely reliant on factories the process is much slower. I remember Steve suggested dip moulding. So, when I went to a dip moulding factory I was looking for these points. I found that they were pretty much answered. The process was as simple to understand as dipping your finger in a pot of

honey. I could see this by doing a simple aluminium sand casting and using it as a test tool. This was cost effective. I also realised that there was an opportunity to make our own test machine in the workshop. I realised we had the ideal process to complement the inflatables, and it offered us a new dimension. Whereas all the inflatable products adopted such a strong inflatable aesthetic, the dip moulding offered the opportunity to be more sensitive with the designs.

The dip moulding would not be as cheap as injection moulding but it had the advantage of tooling costs at a fraction of the price. This meant that commercially it was ideal for volumes from 500 to 50,000. The other advantage it had over injection moulding was that the process of dipping allows the use of excessive undercuts. For anyone who knows a lot about tooling the issues of undercuts play a large part in the decision making of the tooling. This process could do things other processes could not. It was very important to me that we were not just adding another process to the range for the sake of it. I wanted to make sure that it offered a new dimension. The only drawback I could see at the time was the size limitation. Dip moulding is really only cosmetically commercially successful in sizes up to 200 x 200 x 200mm.

The first range with Michael, Steve, Michael, Mark and I was quite an interesting process – there was an interesting response from each of them. One thing I noticed was that it's amazing how definite people work, how they have a way of working. However much you break it down, a lot of their methodology remains.

Steve's the modelmaker and he did some very intricate little models for casting and making dips from. Everything was very fussy and details. Michael Marriott had a fairly clear idea from the start that he wanted to do a vase. It had a wooden base. You couldn't get him away from it and I liked that it was there. Mark was fantastic. He worked how I like to work. He was really interested in the tooling. His tooling was by far the most expensive – 3,500 to 4,000 pounds. I was so impressed with how he had gone about the process. It was so clever, he wasn't drawing a shape and then making it. I had to force him to do a shape once he had the process. He was so wrapped up in how he made it. He wasn't really interested in doing the object. He just wanted to say "Look at that!" He was working on an idea of tooling that was spaced apart in such a way that when dipped everything bonded together.

I was looking at this from a manufacturer's point of view – he's not only brought me a design, but an observation on how you can manipulate a process to gather things you may need. Once you take the principle of that, there's so much more mileage to be got out of it. That, particularly, impressed me. It was my favourite product and it was one of the most successful products. It still sells.

Michael Young was a remarkable character to work with. He was doing good sketches. I had to ad-lib so much from his drawings. As a result we never got it properly.... His product was never as successful as I would have liked it to be. It gave me a weird feeling about being a manufacturer. I learnt a lot as a designer.

There is a different language between designers and manufacturers, and it is the responsibility of the designer to learn the language of the manufacturer. How you communicate to someone. The problem is that the manufacturer is unlikely to learn the language

factory it does tend to drop off quickly. I learnt a lot for myself here, you don't always need to go into a presentation with a sketch, sometimes you want another form of communication... sales figures, whatever. I realised we have to work out what it is... in this project I said I'd manufacture everything... if I was acting more in a directorial role, I would have edited or changed quite a few things. I could see they weren't going to be commercially successful. It's that fine line. If someone's investing 30 grand, there's got to be something in it for them. It's being able to stand back and see it. In amongst it all are pieces that become great sellers. I made some terrible errors with this first dip moulding range. I created a colour pallet of pale blue, yellow and pale green. It did not work well, especially the yellow. As a result I NEVER do anything in yellow now.

In 1997/1998 there was a big shift from plastic to natural materials, and the dip moulding was an interesting process to use as it could look like ceramic, but with a tactile quality. If the first range had been done so as to be more ceramic looking it would have been more successful. But the dip moulding has been, pretty much, a successful range, especially in terms of the commissioned work that came in as a result of all of this.

Various mould samples and tests done in our studio, 1999

Rucksack, 1998
Collaboration Craig Morrison

Soap lounger, 2000
Cross soap tray, 1999
Sink-plunger, 1999
Birdhouse, 2002
Medical pot, 1999
Capsule case, 1998

Virtual Reality

Often you have a vision and then you make the object and the vision isn't fulfilled. Then you change it and you're pleased, but you're then on to the next thing. This rush of computer vision allows us to experience a hyper-real environment. More and more magazines are publishing computer images, and there is a kind of addiction to these hyper-real images. They create a desire which is hard to follow up in reality. Many brands now show computer images of their product, before it is launched, to gauge an idea of the consumer's response. This does not allow for the physical quality of the product.

First test of the Memo seat

Milan, 1999

I had met Ron Arad whilst I was designing my water-proof floating TV, however it was not until I had a call from him inviting me to do a lecture at the RCA that we got talking about this project.

The lecture was one of my worst – there is something about the RCA. Anyway, we agreed to meet in his studio to discuss "an idea he had".

I actually had no clue as to what we were going to discuss and could not work out what he could possibly want with inflatables. The conversation quickly turned to his Transformer seat from the 1980s – he wanted to re-invent it and launch a new version of it. We discussed some of the problems he had discovered doing the Transformer and agreed to work with him on the new project, and see where it take us. Ideally, a launch at Milan 1999 was the aim.

The principle was simple enoug – create an air-tight bag with a valve and some beads inside.

I had already been working with styrene beads, so we had some in the studio. One night I made a sample, which was essentially a sphere 800mm diameter. We sat on it and sucked the beads out, in not believing how well it worked.

Ron and I met a lot over the next few months, developing different versions and sizes of the product. However, Ron had an obsession with the way the valve worked, and its ease of use.

The initial version of the seat had a standard valve, but it was eventually agreed to design and produce a special filling and vacuuming valve for what was now called the Memo.

Going into this project Inflate was financially well positioned, and as a result we were able to invest a lot of money in developing it.

During the course of all this we had to change a lot of the logistical elements of how we worked and made products. Memo, when packed, was big, and as a result we needed to find a new larger packing site, new employees – and we had to build a machine for filling the Memo shells.

Memo was launched in Milan as a pre-production prototype, and was in full production by mid-1999.

Glasgow, 2000

Serpentine, 2000

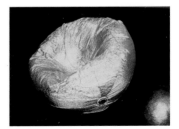

3M reflective Memo, Milan

snoozy

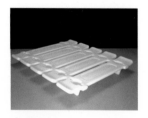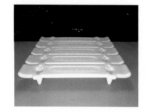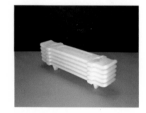

Doing something for the hell of it

One of the things we had been trying to do was a roll-up bed. Some things you can imagine, but you couldn't draw them to save your life. The Snoozy bed was even more out on a limb than other projects. This time it was Paul and I and we were totally unsure about how the whole thing would be received. There's no market testing, none of that goes on, we just make the thing, and then stick one in a show. We were already seven grand down. But the response for the bed was fantastic and had a great impact on how people saw what we were. I learnt a lot from it, it made me recognise that our products didn't have to be funny cuddly things, they could be quite clean and quite serious. The whole thing is very functionally driven, yet has a character to it anyway, inherently through the process that's used to create it. From this moment it's been more about the desire to try to do things that have something of this to them than simply designing product ranges. And that's really why, in the past two years, not much has come out of Inflate. There hasn't been the opportunity or the desire to take certain things through. There have been a lot of completed projects, but we've been doing a lot of stuff for other people. Now we're back to a point where we're looking to do more products – there's a catalogue of ideas built up. In those two years it wasn't like we had no ideas.

Temporary shop, opened in
Selfridges, London 2003. The
shop concept followed on from
Our House at 100% Design. It
was a great opportunity to see
how the brand could work
within a high-brow retail
environment.

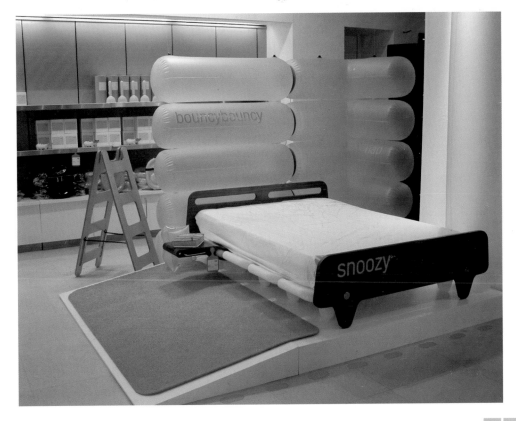

Inflate Shop at Exmouth Market, opened in 2001. It has served as a product development vehicle, as well as a commercial outlet offering the complete product range alongside one-offs and prototypes.

Inflate factory

Inflate studio, 1996-2000

Dish rack, 2003

inflate s2

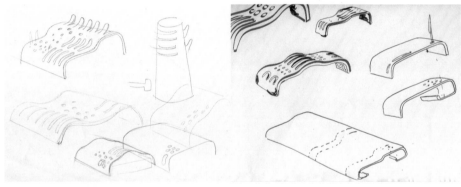

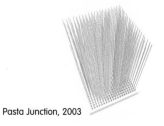

Pasta Junction, 2003

Fold chopping board, 2003

A shared brand

In 2003 I met with a company called S2 solutions. I had been invited to look at the processes they worked with and to see if there were any design opportunities for increasing their commercial offering. S2 solutions work with a material which is a mixture of resin and stone, more commonly known as Corian or Hi Max.

I had met them purely as a consultant within a team led by John Nordon of Idea Architects. However, when I saw the material and the opportunities it offered I quickly realised that there were many commercial opportunites to launch a range of products with this material under the Inflate brand. Ever since setting up the Inflate product range I have always been keen to raise the perceived value of plastic to the consumer.

Along with other consultants, I had been aware of the material for some years (it is actually about 20 years old), but all our memories of trying to work with it were frustrating, as many of the fabricators we had spoken with were not so understanding of the possibilities of using the material in different contexts. S2 solutions were totally open and had the facilities and experience which made the whole process seem as simple as working with MDF.

Within an hour of the initial presentation I was sure of the opportunities of taking the material into new commercial areas. After the initial meetings were complete I decide to approach S2 solutions with the idea of a collaborative range.

The commercial relationship here is as much about potential success as well as design and development. Inflate is responsible for developing the designs and marketing the product. S2 is responsible for prototyping samples and production. All orders are invoiced and distributed direct from their factory. All design and marketing expenses are paid as a percentage of profit. This works well for a tight and competitively priced product – a totally transparent relationship.

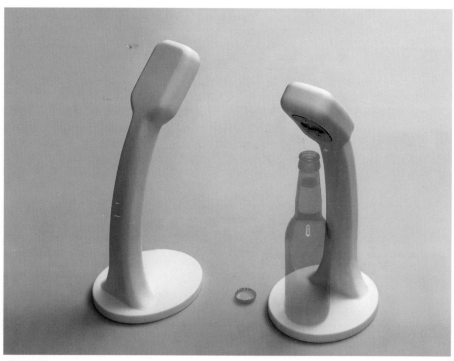

Triffid, 2003

Mug Tree, 2003
Design Peter Rusell Clarke

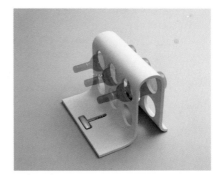

Bottle Rack, 2003

Short Pins Table, 2003
Design Six Wu

Toilet Table, 2003

BIG
STRUCTURES

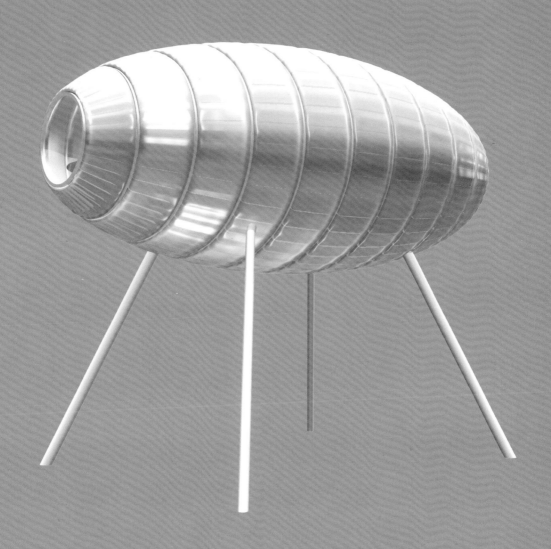

It is all about opening up opportunities: the simple act of designing a component which allows you to do things you couldn't do before....

Before the concept was the project. In 1998 we were commissioned to work on the Swiss Expo 01. The project was to research and develop the creative possibilities of a pneumatic system of components that could be used to create wind barriers on various sites around Lake Geneva. The system was to be designed and presented to a group of short-listed architects for them to use as a tool for their own expression.

I spent one year on the project, investigating different construction techniques for the components that they might offer the most flexibility. This was also the project where I first became involved in the development of larger pneumatic structures using fans and compressors. All of the panels in this type of structure needed to be air powered in some way, and I was beginning to see limitations in this type of building. They needed a lot of 'tube management' for their air supply.

The other thing that struck me was the interfacing between the flexible membranes and the rigid sections. There was often either a compromise in this area or the need for the bespoke construction of connecting devices. Eventually, the project ended with the dismissal of the project director we were working for. Pretty much all the work we had done became worthless. At the time I could not see how this project would benefit us in the future, but then, in 1999, other clients started hovering – the dot.com boom was happening.

So, I was offered three projects which gave me the opportunity to realise three very different approaches to pneumatic structures. As with many ideas these began with a vision of what I wanted to achieve. Air Air was no exception. I was thinking of a monocoque type structure, but the problem was the feasibility of constructing it. It was through the process of investigating how to do this that I came back to the Swiss Expo experience.

The idea of a modular approach was starting to make sense. We undertook a very crude system of creating the structure as a composite of individual panels that would connect together on site to form an enclosure. There were other advantages to the way we were going about our approach here too. We could run cables and lighting through the panels, and in the end the whole thing looked much more impressive at night, as it appeared lit from within.

air air

Air Air was the first modular system that I had worked on, but it was not until working on the Volvo project that I struck on the need for an Air Popper type system. The trouble was, I had always worked with the objective of things being mass produced.

However, when working on larger objects – exhibitions and portable structures – it is more like producing one-offs. And the manufacturing techniques I was familiar with were only suited to producing small numbers of objects. I thought that if I could use these methods to produce multiples of the same object and then tile them together I would be able to build structures as big as we needed. Furthermore, I was also interested in the idea of competitively priced, mass produced large structures. All that was needed was a male and female component that could be used to connect the panels together, allowing air to flow between them. This would reduce the need for multiple fans and/or tubing running all around the structure.

Once the Air Popper component was resolved I could see how useful it was going to be. But one thing I had not considered was the fact that we would have a system of putting together these panels in a way no one else could. We were not only competing with our designs, but at a commercial edge as well. This new system meant we could be a lot more competitive with what we were offering.

In the past these structures would be designed and constructed as single objects. They would be very heavy and the fixings would always be visible, or they would have to use a complicated system of suspended panels. The Air Popper system opened up the opportunity to integrate the framework within the inflatable panels. This gives a very clean look to the structure. In fact, it actually gives the illusion that the whole thing is self-supporting.

The real thing with such a system is that you have to invest in the components before you have any real orders. The design testing and production tooling would have taken around six months to complete. A lot of the projects I am involved in have lead times of as little as one week!

Air Air being installed. The whole design was developed so as to suspend from the existing glass atrium.

Westbourne Studios, 2001

Double Compound, RIBA

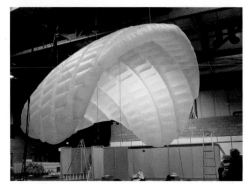

Lecon, Glasgow

Volvo Reveal, Detroit

big m

Taking on more than you can chew

There was another project I was invited to do. This was for a travelling exhibition of digital art. It was to coincide with the millennium and it was conceived as a kind of Dome for the North. The project was called "Big M".

The brief was pretty simple – design and produce a structure that would be suitable to travelling around in a van with three people responsible for setting it up at each venue. And it needed to be set up within half a day. I thought that for this project it would be interesting to work with bouncy castle techniques of manufacture, but to try and come up with a construction that would be more sophisticated in appearance.

The real issue with bouncy castles is the crudeness of their tubes. After visiting a factory which constructs bouncy castles, it was apparent that the only real reason they were constructed in the way they were was to keep their cost as low as possible. As with many manufacturers in the UK, the product is totally price driven and, as a result, all of the factories I visited had edited their offering to the lowest denominator. They all strive for quality of construction, but use the simplest forms. We did not want to make something

more expensive than it needed to be, but I also knew there was the budget with which to push the process.

Bouncy castles are stitched up with a large fan connected to a tube inflating them. During the stitching process it is possible to incorporate slightly differing techniques for constructing the panels. The main difference in what we were proposing was the detail we had put into the panel design. For efficient use of material and the lack of available technology to most manufacturers bouncy castles are built from square panels.

For some time we had been developing all our larger structures through scale models and then using computers for working out the panels exactly. The scale models provided the opportunity to work with a structure in a free manner. Once a design makes sense it is relatively easy to work out the patterns. The development of Big M had resulted in the idea that it would be constructed from three identical panels which would be laced together. Each panel had an entrance/exit. And each panel was designed as a compound form. This required that all of the panels would be tapered and connected using internal

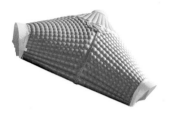

straps. By cutting and spacing the internal straps it was possible to have the panels form a smooth, undulating form. This method of construction has become a blueprint for a lot of our larger work. The only difference now is that we have all of the material laser-cut directly from computer files. The panels can also be marked with stitching guide points.

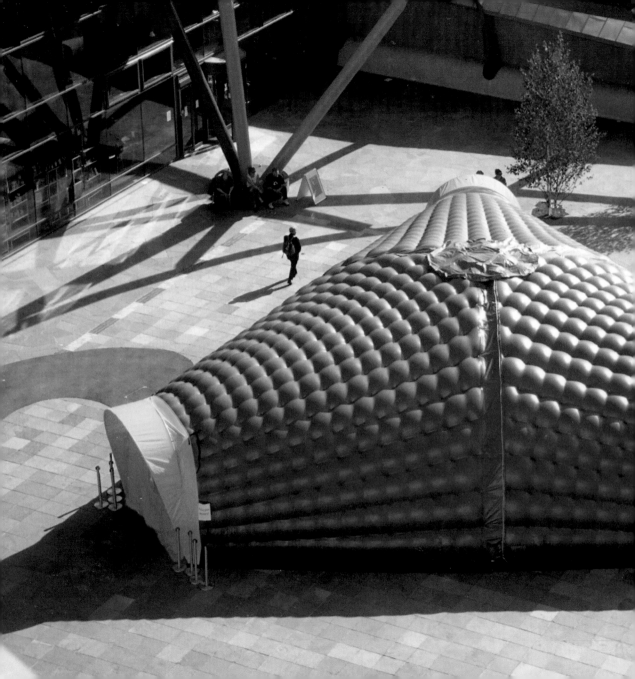

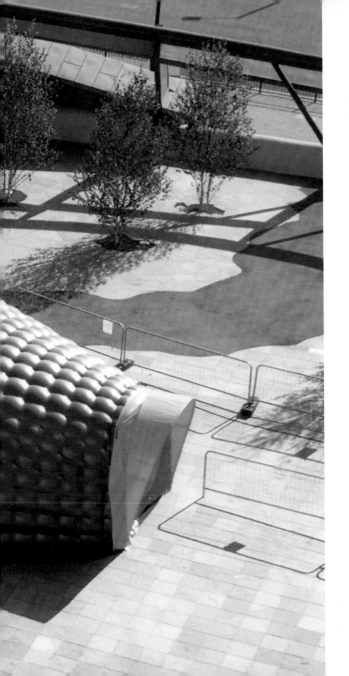

In 2002 I received a phone call and was asked if we could produce a structure 20 metres in diameter? And, if so, how much would it cost? I answered, yes, err, from £30,000. The project was for British Land.

The site would be Broadgate Arena, in London. I knew that for this project we would be using similar principles as those for Big M. But the structure was going to be much bigger – 20 instead of 12 metres. The funny thing with this type of project is that there is a lot of time spent at the start getting a sign-off before you actually start engineering and detailing the work. In any case, the idea was to design a structure as a system of 12 panels which would fit together over an aluminium truss frame. The client specified that there should be no internal columns within the space – i.e. we had to achieve a 20 metre span with no columns. This required a lot of engineering and, surprisingly, a lot more calculating in getting the wind deflection and uplift taken care of. In a strange way, for a project which took six months of intensive work, the end result is rather simple to explain. Once all of the design had been resolved we began the build. The panels were going to be constructed in a similar way to those for Big M. This time we were also working with a sailmaker from

Southampton on the construction. All the metalwork was being made in London. The plan was for everything to come together for the event in September 2002. Then, a couple of weeks before the event I received another call explaining that everything had been cancelled. We had already been pretty much paid so this was not a problem. The real issue was that we had put six months of most of the studio's time into developing this project and we had not been allowed to PR our work. In the end we reached an agreement with the client to keep the structure and look for rental possibilities for it. At the time we had actually been discussing the rental side of the business.

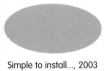    

Simple to install..., 2003

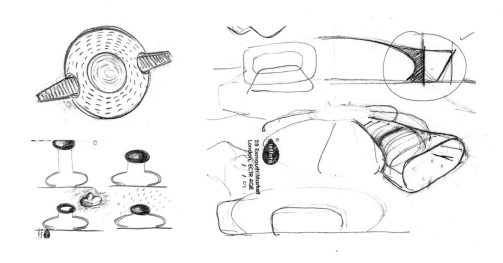

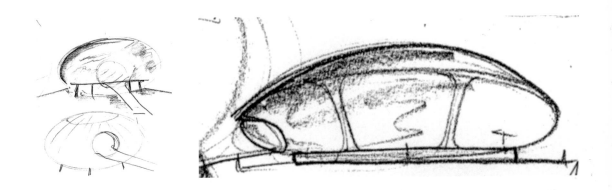

28 Exmouth Market
London, EC1R 4QE

o2

sitooterie

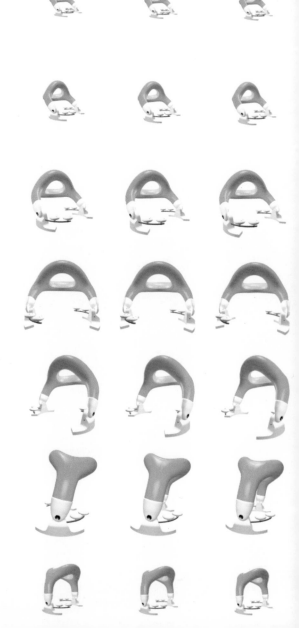

The idea behind this design was to develop a structure that was not all enclosed, but would offer protection against the wind and rain. The result was a structure that could be moved from one side to another. I also wanted to work with a combination of materials and used the air moulding to create croncrete seats to anchor the structure whilst using a light weight material for the roof.

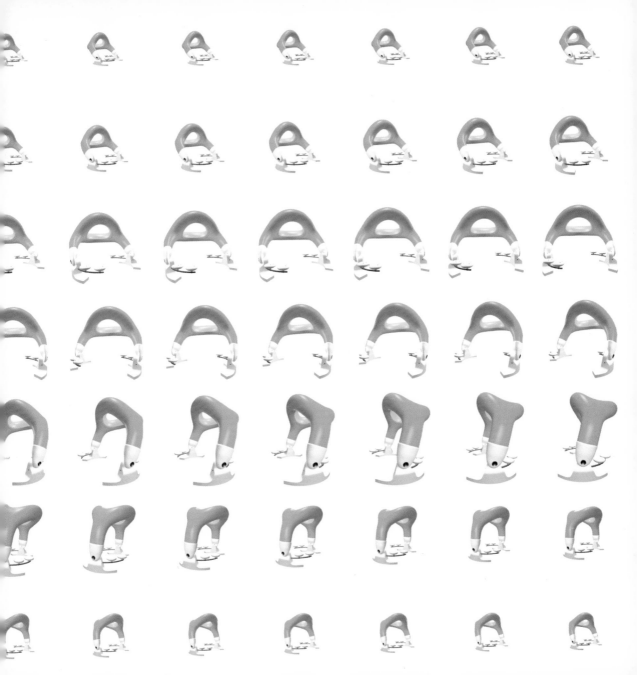

Air moulding – moving from product to mould

I have had a fascination with concrete since experimenting with it at college. I also spent many summers laying cement foundations for my Dad. I had wanted to get back into the concrete idea but time was tight with all the other projects we were experimenting with. Anyway, we somehow did a load of tests using inflatables to make concrete form – that is, using the inflatables as moulds.

There are two basic ways of working here. The first is to make an inflatable form and cast concrete on or around it. The other is to make a mould and fill it with concrete, seal it and pump the mould up casting the concrete inside. This is the technique we used for the air moulded interior concept. It is also the technique used later in the Poole Harbour project.

This was a test we did which shows an interior environment. We were basically creating a negative space. Again, we didn't quite know what was happening. We were at the mercy of what was going on inside the mould – it being inflated and stretched. And there's this lovely seam. I couldn't see much commercial future in all this at the time. The concrete was so heavy that I realised we would need to work on architecturally scaled projects. It became a suspended idea.

But a couple of years ago I revisited the idea with the notion of producing air moulded fibreglass bathroom objects. The thought here was of production customisation. The moulds were relatively cheap to produce and they would all be slightly different. Unfortunately, the bathroom idea did not make it past a few small prototypes. However, lately we have produced a couple of one-off shower cubicles using these techniques.

Air moulded interior, 1999

Air moulded concrete BBQ, 2002

Concrete landscape, 2003

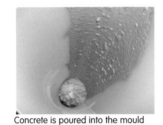

Concrete is poured into the mould

The mould is then inflated

Outer air chambers are inflated to deform the inner concrete

The mould is carefully suspended and left to set for 12 hours

The mould is cut from the concrete

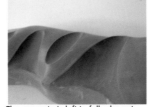

The concrete is left to fully dry out

In 2002 Jerszy Seymour approached me to work with him on a concept for spraying PU foam over inflatables to make an exhibition space. The thing that struck me about this project was the material used. It was sprayed on the inflatable and set in ten seconds. It was light-weight. The PU foam provided us with the opportunity to explore the air moulding idea at a large scale. The result of this collaboration was a space somewhere around 20 x 10 meters. It was a concept piece. We simply built a number of big spheres and these were inflated two at a time and placed touching each other. Foam was then sprayed over them and once it had set the inflatables were deflated and the process repeated until the whole structure was complete. Where the spheres touched, these became the walkways from one space to another. The detailing was crude, but the result was stunning in a strange sort of way and it was all made in a day and a half. Working on this project gave me the opportunity to look at all the air moulding I had been involved with again. I realised that there was this opportunity to combine all the materials to create a quick build house concept.

Take an inflatable hemisphere.

Reverse stick on all plugs light fittings, etc..

Cover the whole lot in fibreglass, leaving the backs of the fittings accessible.

Wire everything up.

Spray with foam.

Spray with concrete.

Deflate and go inside.

One quick build house!

foamo

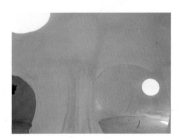

flood

I was invited to produce a design for a 'house of the future'. I didn't want to just do a fancy looking house.

There had been a number of earthquakes in the media that year – Turkey and China... and there had been increased flooding as well. I was trying to use bad luck in a way that something good might come out of it. The news is always about disasters. We always think it's about other people... and often it is.

But, these things can effect all of us, you know. We live in London and think "It'll never happen to us." But it could happen to anyone. Then, I thought, why do these events have to be 'disasters'? Why can't they be seen as opportunities? Ok, you can't do much about an earthquake when it happens, but the ideas around Flood have to do with trying to put a positive outlook on these situations. What usually happens with a disaster is the army comes in and bulldozes a massive flat areas of land and concretes it. They then stick up big tents as emergency housing – the beginnings of a shanty town. Some people have to stay in these places for up to a year. But it doesn't have to be like this. I don't think it should be like this. That was the basis for the flood structure, to create a component that would be modular. You could plug

them together. Each one was comfortable for two or three people and you could put everything in it, even though it wasn't massive. Then, if you had a big family, you could join them together and create this web. There would be enforced recreational areas between private space, or you could create semi-private space, or disjoin them and create totally public space. Let's not create shanty towns. Think about the people.

The main thing here is it would come as a flat-pack. The other thing I was really into was my way of paying for it. Normally in a disaster, you need money instantly. I thought of making a structure that people would buy and use regardless, like in their garden as a conservatory, or an extension. I like the idea that you create something that would be funded by the private sector, people would own it, but they would buy it under license and in the event of a disaster they would be packed down and sent to wherever. People would then be reimbursed or given a new one. You're using the planet as your storage system – you have them everywhere. If you owned one and you were caught in an earthquake, you would be a priority. Like an insurance policy. So people that live in a risk area would buy one as an insurance policy.

Another thing with Flood is that it can float. So if the whole area is flooded you can float around in the city.

Many of the projects we get involved with only require that the structure be used for a short period of time. And most clients are put off by the development costs in having a bespoke design done for them. This led to something of the thinking behind the development of Office in a Bucket (OIAB).

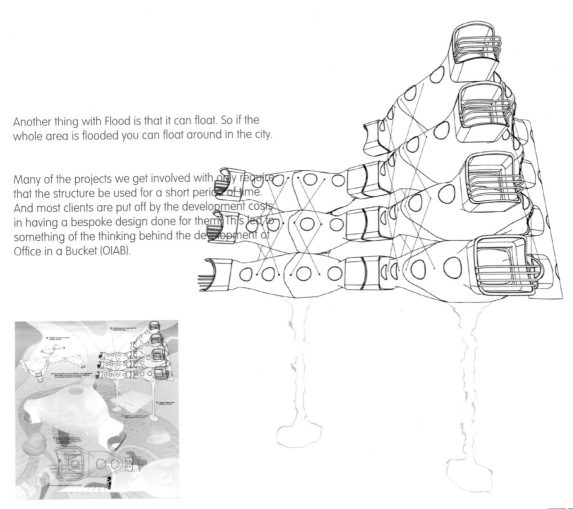

Buckets of fun was designed as a children's toy concept for a project in Homes and Gardens, 2001.

Working with ripstop nylon allowed for a totally different approach to creating large inflatables structures. The material is very light and very strong, allowing for the design and production of self-supporting structures which pack down very small when not used, making them easy to transport and store.

Arco portable exhibition structure, 2001

oiab

Creating a product for a problem which does not exist.

Concept – "Any idiot can set it up. If you know how to use a bucket, then you should be able to use this."

Having done exhibitions and events for the last seven years, I knew that the hardest thing was to develop and produce a product that was simple to set up and durable enough for anyone to be able to use over a period of time. Being inside a pneumatic structure is fantastic. What got me thinking more about this idea was the work we did for Volvo a few years ago. This was a car cover for one of their launch events. We spent a lot of time inside this thing building it. It was a complicated structure. Outside the client was driving me up the wall, but when I went inside the structure, everything was tranquillity! Sound was deadened and no one knew where you were. The problem here was that I knew most people wouldn't want to pay for the product development of such an object, so I decided to try and create something which could become an off-the-shelf product.

Office in a Bucket is really a combination of editing out and developing a clean system that captures the essence of privacy, whilst embracing some of the problems I thought potential clients might have with such a structure. For me this is "form follows constraint".

The OIAB thing is about buying and owning a product like this, having it available to you and it not taking up loads of storage space, but being big when it's inflated. That's what is so magic about it – being kept in a little bucket and then it can become a four by five meter room! It's a bit like a parachute – you jump out of a plane and out it comes from a little rucksack on your back. It's that kind of sensation.

The door, though, was an issue, coming in and going out. There was initially this idea that there would be a zip up the front, but I was not convinced by this. I felt it might seem a little claustrophobic. Another concern and a common question I get is "What happens if it deflates?" So, we decided to remove the roof from the centre of the structure and have the outer walls curve such that from outside it looks enclosed, but when inside you have a skylight, and openness. This works well, in another way too, as you don't need integral lighting. I completed the design so that it opens and closes like a clam, eliminating the need for the door. The great thing is, you've got this bucket and there's the structure and a fan at the bottom of the bucket. The structure is connected to the bucket and it just inflates. Use it and just pack it in the bucket when you are finished with it.

Office in a Bucket, 2003

Structure comes out

and

inflates in eight minutes

ready to use.

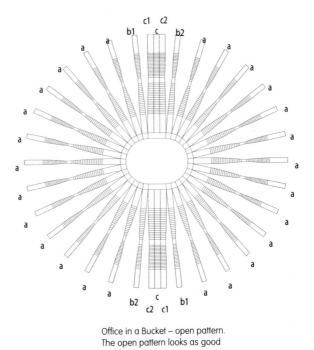

Office in a Bucket – open pattern.
The open pattern looks as good
as the final object.

Having developed the Office in a Bucket, it
became apparent that the concept could
be developed further into a shop in a van.

toys

The OBE toy is a concept design for a child building game. It has functional similarities to Meccano.

I had been thinking about doing it for some time. Originally the idea was to use the Air Popper system to create a series of building blocks which could be connected together to make different structures when inflated. There are many inflatable kids' toys on the market, but very few which offer the possibility to explore building. I have always enjoyed the hands on approach, and I believe it is whilst young we gain these tendencies.

Having a young child had taught me how basic the thing really needed to be. I did some sketches of potential components, and then I totally edited it down. I was going to work out the patterns and make the whole thing. I wanted to be able to manufacture the entire kit in one day.

It was now five years since the Expo project, where I had been working on an architectural scale system of inflated components. The budget had been massive and all it ended up in was a political nightmare. I did take a lot of experience from all this, especially the opportunities there were for inflatable systems. The toy had to be as simple as possible and eventually I edited it down to three components:

One straight – these act as rods in friction between the panels.

One panel, with holes in – this can be used with the concertina and the straight.

One concertina – this acts very much like a nut and bolt, but works in compression.

I made ten of each of the components. I was not sure how it was going to work, or how excited my son would be. I decided to give it all to him wrapped up and to film him opening the present and to photograph the sequence of putting it together with him. It only took 30 minutes to build a couple of configurations without ever having used it before. With some further development I can see a lot of mileage in the concept. I look at it and think... I could make more components. I've got some ideas, like measures on a ruler, so you can go and measure things. On the other components there'll be numbers and colour coding. So you get this idea of what a

The brief was simple – a 300mm square block of foam, a scalpel and a sheet of sandpaper – create a toy design which could be auctioned for a child's charity.

My idea was to create a 3-D puzzle, which when constructed properly held all the pieces together in a single object.

component is. There are curves and… the idea is to make a sort of 3-D connector that allows you to go out in many directions.

I wouldn't do the OBE toy with Inflate, the toy industry is too big. There are no small time people who make it. I would rather make less money and be in the position of getting it out to more people in a format that makes sense, than producing it myself and being copied by someone else. You then only have to adjust it a bit… invariably, if you think you've come up with the best system and then it's adjusted, it can be made worse. My biggest fear with the OBE toy is that someone's going to turn around and say, "It's done." I thought, it's so simple, so obvious…, but then I thought, no, there are things to this that I've done that have come through a lot of experience. I always say in the studio that if we sit down and just draw shapes someone will have already done it. What you're trying to do is create a kind of argument in a product form. I think the OBE toy for me is my argument that you could do it, this could be it. It comes from truly understanding something....

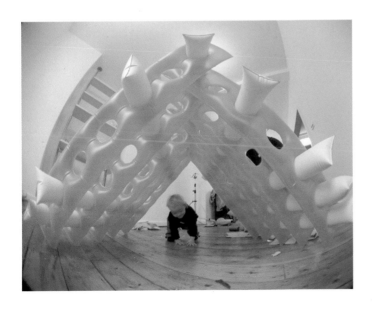

Inflatable greenhouse concepts, 2003

I met Catherine Finlay through a project we were working on with her for Claydon Healy. We were essentially producing some elements of the project for them. Catherine is a very energetic person with more ideas than there is space on the table, and we got on pretty well, because of our mutual interest in materials. This allowed for great freedom of expression. Catherine mentioned that she had this project to do a room for the future, for Homes and Gardens. We agreed to collaborate. I was determined to keep it as sane as possible, knowing the problems architects can create with such projects. It was unpaid and needed discipline.

Catherine had recently been doing a lot of work with bamboo, and just happened to have a lot left over. I happened to have a lot of PVC. We did quite a few experiments which led to the final concep, which was basically to weave together two materials, the bamboo and inflatable tubes. The structure was really tough. It was a 200 metre tube weaving all the way through a coil of bamboo. The whole thing was set up with the tube deflated. The coils could be pulled or compressed to form different volumes. Once we were happy with a form the tube was inflated to a highish pressure, which knitted the whole thing into a rigid form.

It has one pump pumping it up to a high pressure. You can see the bamboo is woven in such a way that you can pull the structure and have it long and thin or you can prise it together and have it short and fat. You can deflate it, push it to how you want to change it and then inflate it.

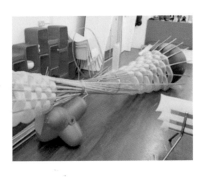

STUDIO

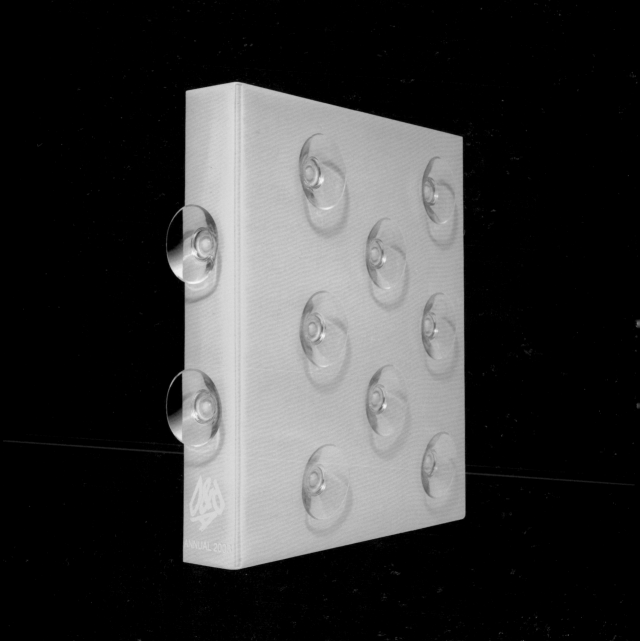

ANNUAL 2003

I am not sure when the studio actually came into being. The brand definitely came first. The thing was that I actually learnt so much through the development of the brand that I thought there was an opportunity to build a studio and consultancy alongside it. So, I have never worked in another studio. I have developed my own ideas as to how I see a studio. I am happy with this, even though it may appear to be a little chaotic at times. The way I judge it is by the type of work that is produced through it.

In the last eight years I have overseen a company which has developed a brand from nothing, on a very small budget and with no outside investment. Our projects have ranged from small packaging design through to architecturally scaled 'buildings'. An additional angle has been the production side of the company. The experiences of developing products for the brand meant that we built up a strong manufacturing base.

I now very much understand the relationship between these two parts of the business. The studio is able to offer its creative services through to production and delivery. We can now even offer fulfilment and distribution. The core of this is that we can maximise the creative potential for our clients throughout production. Our services are used a lot by other design studios to help them creatively realise projects for their clients. Many of these clients do not wish for us to be credited, which is fine, we just charge more. Other clients we build lasting relationships with where we work together to win more work.

I have always insisted that we invest profits from our bigger projects back into the studio. Some clients are happier to pay for the product and not the design. For these clients we offer an all-in-package which gives us exclusivity on the production rights in a pre-agreed financial structure. I believe people should be financially rewarded. However, the design industry is not like banking.

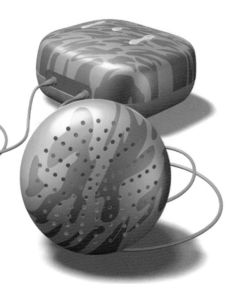

My personal way of working is very much from physical drawing. I enjoy the different emotions that can be applied through the pencil, rather than the singular standardisation of the computer. Don't get me wrong, computers have their place. It is probably because I just missed out on the leap in computer technology at college. I think the year just after mine was when things started to be much more accessible. The way I use computers now is simple: I do a sketch on a piece of paper. I can then take a digital picture which I down load to my laptop. This can then be e-mailed. I am not very good at downsizing the images in PhotoShop, so I tend to have to send lots of e-mails with attachments. In the studio we do a lot of computer visuals, but where possible the work is done through 3-D models or sketching. The computer is really for resolving the design when the idea is formulated. My new design for a computer is as a door stop. In the past few years I have had three die on me. The screens just seem to go blank.

Plug and Play amp and speakers, 2003

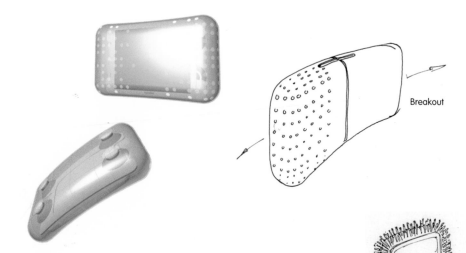

Breakout

Spike

THE
GRASS
IS ALWAYS
GREENER.

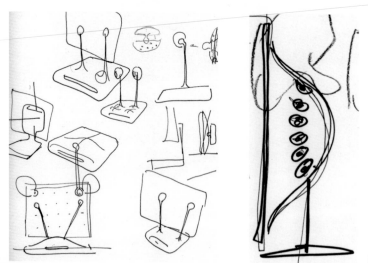

Plug and Play

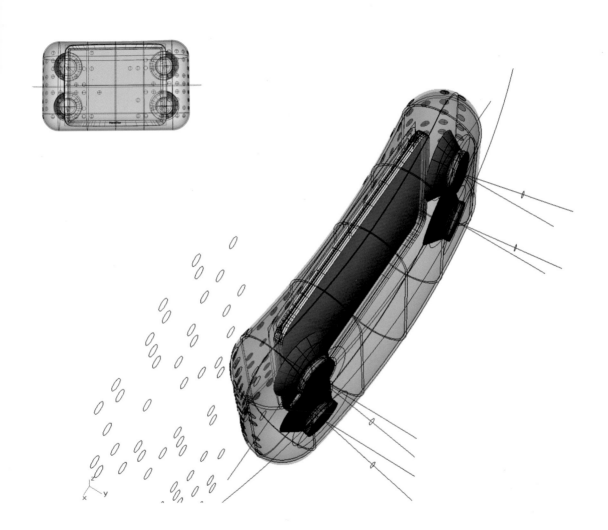

plug and play

The main idea behind the product was to create something that would become a part of the furniture. Too many electrical objects are designed around the idea of how many functions they can incorporate. I always find this annoying, as all I want is for the thing to work well. A TV is something to look at, when on as well as off. I like the idea that it can sit in the corner like a table lamp.

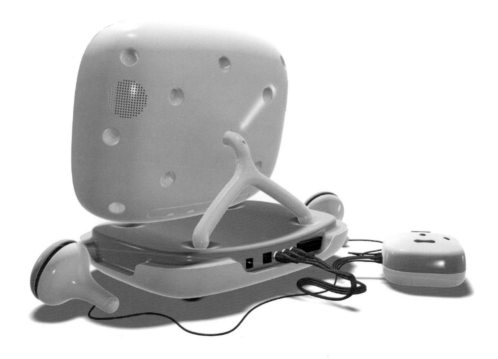

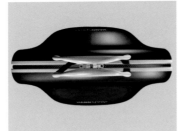

TV bags, 2003

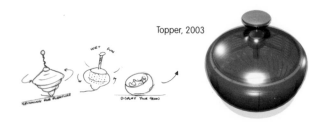

Topper, 2003

My approach to smaller objects has always been about developing ideas through process. Of course, it is necessary to have the brief and requirements from the client. But I like working through ideas on and off. I like to have lots of things on the go all the time. This can be especially useful when people require some ideas quickly.

What makes us different: it is something inside. It's hard to resolve what is right and what is wrong. If you sat down and took away everything you know about people and just let them discuss how they approach things, you'd find that there'd be a lot of common ground – something they can't describe. This takes them down their own unique route.

I remember when Jasper and Ron were doing this whiskey project. It was a funny old situation. Ron is always looking for the idea – he always says he likes to identify an idea, and once he has the idea he likes to go with it. I was looking at what he and Jasper had done, and really they had started from a similar point. It was more about the idea of what they were trying to do – Jasper's was done in his way and Ron's was done in his. They each retained an element of elegance and simplicity. They hadn't become fussy

or complicated. But to Ron what wasn't fussy and complicated to Jasper was terribly fussy and complicated. It's how you see cleanness – the art of closing the projects rather than the art of opening it.

How do you commercialise the design process? When you're working on a project you have such an amazing overview of experiences gathered, that you harness them subconsciously. Imagine doing it with no information! If a client wants something very specific, you need to be narrowing-in. At other times you need to be looking out, embracing other things. The reality is, if you get a duff negative brief from a client, if you harness it well you can be very interesting.

How projects evolve is fascinating. It's remarkable how something so simple... I could probably talk to you for about three days about the inflatable OBE toy. At the end I've probably got the most basic of inflatable objects. It's like Starck said: "It takes three seconds to design an object." What he's neglected are the previous 45 years that influenced that three seconds. With Dyson, they said he made his fortune in three years, but it's actually 14 years plus three years. We love to edit and glamorise.

Magnetic peg, 2000

There should be a law saying "Because you do this for a living, by law, you can't buy your child any toys, you have to design him something!"

There are two things really – a product like the OBE toy comes from ideas over a few years. I thought I've never designed anything for Obe and he's nearly two. I thought right, the OBE toy is it. I thought of all the problems in detail and then had a moment of clarity, you strip out all the rubbish and if you look at the system, it's nothing.

I have a strong belief that if you lose the thing you start with, it's like a plant, if you cut the roots, it dies. With the welders, I had to get it here at the studio because without it, the soul and sprit of our work has been taken away. It's not the be all and end all, but I've tried to explain to clients that my thinking is an outlet for a range of thoughts and this became successful and became a business in its own right. The thing that was most key, was learning the value of experimentation. That's what the studio space is about. To just let things happen, no phones, no interruptions.

Twisted hip flask, 1999
(for Glenlivet)

Coathangers, 1999
(for Future Systems)

Boots, 1999

Pod Shoes, 1999

Over the years I have been involved in hundreds of packaging products. The thing I really enjoy about this type of work is when I can get involved turning the packaging into a product in its own right. If we have packaging it should have a function, if not why have anything other than a basic protective layer.

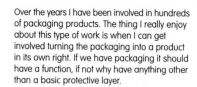

Boots, 1999

Maltesers, 2003

Creation Records, 2000

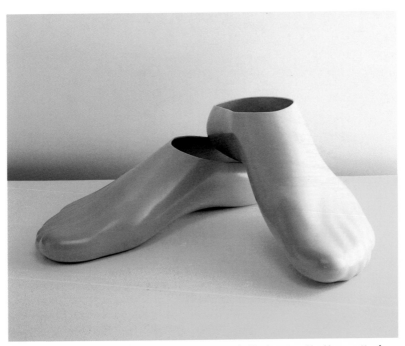

I had been wanting to do something by creating a dip mounded body part, and had been waiting for the right opportunity for this. When I met Michico Koshino I realised my opportunity had come along. We were working on a range of inflatable dresses for her, so I suggested the dip molded foot idea and it became part of the show.

For these shoes we simple made a plaster cast of Fiona's feet and then had an aluminium replica tool made. This was then used to produce a limited edition.

national service

Teaching should be run as a national service. Everyone should be expected to re-invest two years of their life back into the system. Ever since I graduated from the RCA I thought about giving something back.

I eventually got involved with teaching after Ron asked me to do a lecture at the RCA.

I was not a model student whilst at the college, and I thought that I could go back and teach with this and help those who were... like me.

I think I could have done more at college if I'd understood what the school offered. I understood enough to get a lot out of it, but I didn't understand what an MA was all about. It was only when I left that I did.

The problem for me, and I feel for many other RCA students, is that you think you have made it by being accepted to the college. But you don't fully commit to taking part in what the college has to offer. I think I would have benfited much more if there were a clearer message being sent out that you are not yet a success, but have to work towards this.

In a way, the RCA has become a brand that designers want to be associated with, but do not always want to give something to. I'm always looking to see who's coming through. That was a definite draw to working at the RCA no one is in it for the money, and as a result we can be quite outspoken at times. I think it is important to be able to push the students.

At BA level things are all a bit too nice, and as a result the general standard of students is getting wetter – they are not used to hard criticism... and if they cannot handle it at college then what will happened to them, and the future of our industry, in the real world.

The other thing I have done is the Vitra Summer School. This fits in with my desire to eventually open up a professional school abroad, somehow linked to industry. I ran Inflate like a college when we set up, as there was nothing else to emulate, I'd never worked in such an environment before.

I've tried to retain that. Going back to teaching makes me realise we haven't moved that far from college... mentally we're tuned in to recognise the potential that exists in people. I always say to the students

I was working on an exhibition design called Dirty Washing, which was to be made from 1,000 sheet of cardboard. There was going to be a lot of off-cuts so I took the opportunity to test a concept I had for a folding sofa bed.
Even though the cardboard has a great look in its own right the durability of producing it in plastic makes a lot more sense. Actually thinking about it this could be a good RCA project!

who complain that they can't do things that there's so much here in the workshops, etc., and it's not until you leave that you understand how much. That's one thing that I realised when I left – how much was missing from what I took for granted.

Students can be so taken in by magazines and press stuff that they want to be pop stars before the graft. It's like the 'popstars' programme on telly. People think that you can just make it without earning your stripes.

I have invested three years back into the system and I am still enjoying it. As long as this is the case I will carry on.

After all, I hope I am not in the business of educating the only the design-led consumers of the future....

The Mag table is a concept design taking a different approach to the nest of tables. By having individual units which magnet together the opportunity arose to have a table where bits could be broken off to became separate tables and also turn around to create different functions, such as magazine holders.

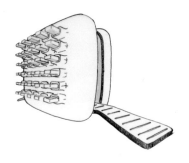

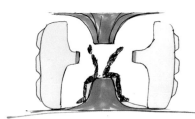

This project has no purpose here other than reminding me of the ones that get away. I was invited by the ad agency Mother to pitch for a launch project for Xelibri mobile phones. The first presentation went really well, however the final meeting to propose our ideas was met with silence and the only comment was, "Did we read the brief." Yes, but clearly something had changed.

Maybe it was the idea of buildings cracking in half with their contents flowing into the road – a form of yolk. Or maybe the Mork and Mindy link was not picked up on. I think they just wanted a display case.

The small Dirty Objects project began in the back
streets of Hong Kong. In one of the shops there I
found two really nice dustpan and brush sets. It got
me thinking about the idea of cleaning, and when
we returned to the studio we began discussing it a
bit more.

Dusty is a simple dustpan and brush, with the idea being to create
a design that suggested a sweeping action – when dusting is
complete the two components seal together holding the rubbish
inside.

dirty objects

Moppit has a couple of things going for it, however the main idea was the action and design of the 'tentacles' – it is the tentacles that are most fun. The design incorporates a system of sponge balls, wrapped within a tight platic net mesh. The balls are of different densities, with the net encapsulating them acting as an abrasive, releasing dirt from the floor.

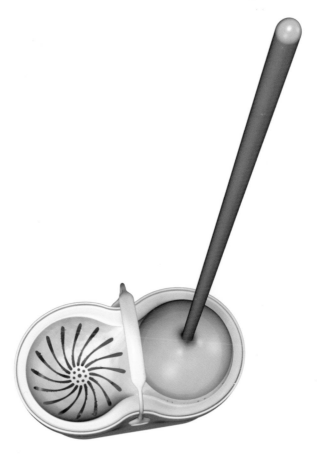

smallGLOBAL is hard to describe, however in simple terms it is a 'virtual company'.

The idea of virtual companies has been around for a long time, but it was not until the widespread use of high speed internet connections that the whole thing started to become a reality. Everything is moving so fast – it is now quicker to e-mail a colleague in the same building than to deal with s/he in person. So why be in the same building?

Having been involved in a number of large scale projects, such as with the Millennium Experience Company, I have seen the inefficiencies and problems in delegating creative thinking over a broad area. I've often felt that my services were not being used to best effect in these situations.

I had been discussing these issues and my feelings on the subject with John Nordan from Idea Architects, and we got onto the idea of a virtual company. I suggested that he should also meet with Jamie, from JAM. After a few meetings John came up with the name smallGLOBAL. It stuck.

John was keen that we become genuinely global, and as a result Mark Dytham, based in Japan, also became a founding partner.

As with all good ideas, it is not until you actually start to do something that the thing has any value. The first project we went for was the redevelopment of Blackpool Pier. We didn't get it. Our second pitch was for the redevelopment of Poole Harbour. As we made it through, stage by stage, we realised that smallGLOBAL was starting to work. Finally, we won the project.

The brief was to create a master plan outlining the development work for Poole over the next 15 years. The scheme involves public and private consultation, aiming to show all parties how, in creatively joining together their commercial and social concerns, a way forward can be found for all.

smallglobal

The whole range covers all items from tree grates to main road illumination. We wanted to create objects that would give Poole its own unique identity.

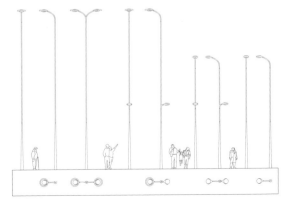

This range of street furniture has been developed with Tim Stolzenburg and John Nordon.

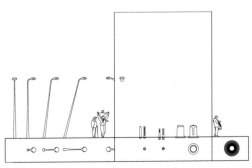

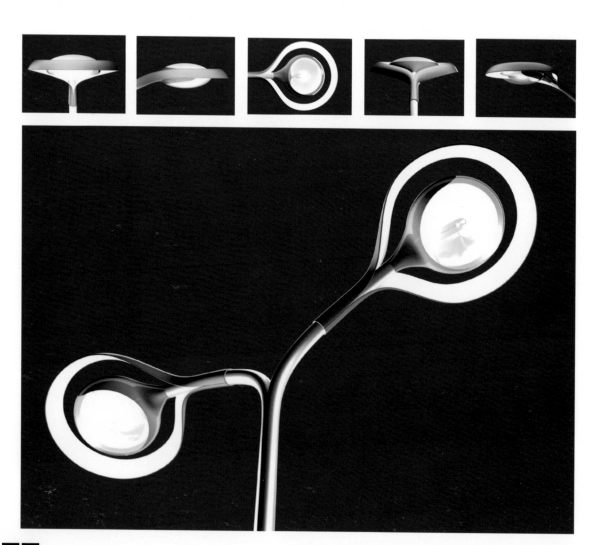

Street Bollards with internal lighting to illuminate pedestrian walkways. These are unassuming but peel away to reveal a light.

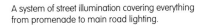

A system of street illumination covering everything from promenade to main road lighting.

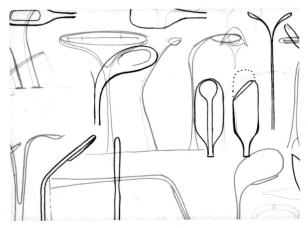

smallGLOBAL is a community of like minded individuals who are all directors of their own enterprises. Each company represents a unique business. These companies came together as smallGLOBAL to work on projects with the potential to transform social and environmental conditions. For every project they create a bespoke team to co-ordinate and implement strategic solutions.

ACKNOWLEDGMENTS

My Mum who has worked with me since the beginning and has taken a lot from me particulary when I am stressed. Now, though, I think she mainly comes in for the grandchildren.

Fiona has been a good friend of mine for nearly 20 years and after a phone call in 1998 she became an important part of the studio. Her background at Red or Dead has served well in developing the Inflate brand, and more recently bringing new business concepts to the studio.

I phoned Larry first in 1995, to help with the production of some of the first inflatable products. Since then we have developed a much closer relationship, which has been crucial to how my career has developed, but I also hope he has learnt something from our journey so far.

Tim has been working with me for two years now. His commitment and loyalty in the last year has been unquestionable. We have more recently been working together closely on all aspects of design – the S2 products, TV and, more recently, we have been developing production techniques for larger scale projects.

Duncan joined in the middle of the O2 project, and has been working flat out since. He brings humour to the studio, and a very tasty creamy salmon sauce to your home.

Special Mention

Paul Crofts worked with me from 1997 to 2003. He has recently set up his own studio – I don't think he is doing inflatables! In reading this book, anything from 1998 to 2003 would have an element of Paul's hand in it somewhere, particulary the Snoozy and much of the exhibition work.

This book has been therapy. I have been through a lot since we began discussing it back in 2001. Most notably, I have been married and have two great kids.

The business has had its ups and downs. The fallout from the dot.com boom had a lingering effect, and it has really taken until now to overcome this.

The current studio is a solid loyal bunch.

For me working through this book has been a lot about realising how much influence and help I have had from other people. The loyalty over the last few months has allowed us to produce what I feel has been the best work the studio has ever achieved.

As I look back it is good to see how our ideas have developed and the investment in self-intiated projects has enriched what we have to offer to our clients.

In the world we now work within there is not enough time to develop ideas on a project by project basis. It is necessary for us to be developing and creating potential solutions and ideas in anticipation of a problem.

For me working with a physical process to develop ideas has a magic and surprise about it. I can remember someone saying to me 1995, "When do you think you will stop doing inflatables?" I had no desire to stop then, as I thought there was still a lot to discover through the process – and I feel there is even more now.

Hopefully, by reading through the book you will see that it is not all about inflatables, but there is a principle and process which follows through from project to project.

If I am not surprised and excited about a project, then why should I expect anyone else to be.

This book has surprised me.

2004 will see Inflate become a stand alone brand with a production facility, supported by the current studio.

Fiona, Tim and myself have plans to develop a new generation consultancy, launching new brands to complement Inflate, whilst embracing the smallGLOBAL philosophy to build them.

I would like to thank everyone involved in this book, especially Emilia Gómez López and Alexander Payne.

Thank you to Catherine, Oberon and Ottilie for allowing me to be an absent father during all this.

inside back cover
Sheppard Robson carnival float, 2003